Beaufort Sea

ALASKA

FAIRBANKS

Mt. McKinley

PALMER
MATANUSKA
ANCHORAGE
VALDEZ
CORDOVA

SEWARD

Cook Inlet

Alaska Highway

SKAGWAY

JUNEAU

PETERSBURG

SITKA

WRANGELL

KETCHIKAN

GULF OF ALASKA

Kodiak Island

Attu Island

BERING SEA

Aleutian Islands

Andreanof Islands

Kiska Island

PACIFIC OCEAN

LIFE IN AMERICA
ALASKA

by Stuart R. Tompkins

Dr. Stuart R. Tompkins is a well-known historian and a member of the Society of American Historians. He is the author of books and numerous articles on Alaska. For some years he served in the history departments of the University of Oklahoma and the University of California. The time that he spent in Alaska qualified him to write about this new state in a very interesting manner.

EDITORS AND ADVISORS

Curriculum Editor	Raymond E. Fideler
Associate Editor	David Proud
Manuscript Editors	Mary Jane Fowler
	Diane Kirkpatrick
	Marilyn Zylstra
Picture Editor	Diane Kirkpatrick
Index Editor	Hester Chase
Art Editor	Alan Adsmond
Map Editors	Ruth Wieda
	Mamie Witbeck
Geographical Editor	Kirk H. Stone,
	Professor of Geography,
	University of Wisconsin

LIFE IN AMERICA

NEW ENGLAND	**THE GREAT PLAINS**
THE NORTHEAST	**THE WEST**
THE MIDWEST	**ALASKA**
THE SOUTH	**HAWAIIAN ISLANDS**

LIFE IN AMERICA
ALASKA

By Stuart R. Tompkins

THE FIDELER COMPANY—GRAND RAPIDS, MICHIGAN

Grateful acknowledgment is made to the following for permission to use the photographs found in this book:

Alaska Life Publishing Company: Page 43.
Alaska Railroad: Page 100.
Annette Islands Canning Company: Page 67.
Black Star: Pages 16, 18, 27, 34, 39, 64, 88, and 90.
Brown Brothers: Pages 42, 73, 74, 83, 97, 98, 99, 119, and 121.
Combine Photos, Ltd.: Page 26.
Galloway: Pages 11, 17, 20, 21, 22, 29, 36, 38, 40, 44, 46, 63, 65, 70, 71, 81, 82, 86, 92, 112, and 116.
Gendreau: Pages 9, 23, 62, and 72.
Greany, Juneau: Pages 113 and 117.
Ketchikan Pulp Company, Ketchikan: Page 25.
Keystone View Company: Page 69.
Mac's Foto Service, Anchorage: Pages 41, 78, 80, 85, 95, 103, and 108.
Northern Consolidated Airlines: Page 104.
Northern Radio Company: Page 102.
Northwest Orient Airlines: Page 94.
Pan American World Airways: Page 120.
Pix, Incorporated: Page 105.
Rapho Guillumette: Pages 58, 59, 60, and 101.
Roberts: Pages 3, 12, 14, 19, 24, 47, 52, 68, 93, and 118.
Sawders: Page 77.
Three Lions: Pages 45, 50, and 87.
Underwood & Underwood: Page 89.
U. S. Army: Page 28.
U. S. Department of the Interior: Pages 37 and 48.
U. S. Fish and Wildlife Service: Pages 30, 31, 32, 35, 49, 53, 54, 55, 56, 57, 61, 66, 76, 79, 84, and 107.
U. S. Forest Service: Pages 10, 33, and 111.
University of Alaska, College: Page 110.
Wells, Anchorage: Pages 15, 51, 114, and 115.
Wien Alaska Airlines: Page 106.

A Better Way to Study Alaska

1. Use five to ten copies of this *Life in America: Alaska* book and one copy of the *Alaska* portfolio of Classroom Pictures (loose-leaf edition of the book) to interest the class in learning more about Alaska and the people who live there. The students will naturally ask many questions.

2. Divide the class into five committees, each of which will seek answers to such questions as:

   . . . What are the people of Alaska like?
   . . . What are the land and climate of Alaska like?
   . . . How do the people of Alaska make a living?
   (See list of chapters in this book.)

3. For its research work, let each committee use traditional textbooks and one or more copies of the *Alaska* book, plus those chapters and pictures from the *Alaska* portfolio that relate to the topic the committee is investigating. This easy-to-understand text, enriched with well-chosen pictures for each topic, makes learning much more effective. It speeds up the learning process and makes the students feel that they are being transplanted in imagination to Alaska.

4. Then let each committee present its most important findings to the class. The committee should be questioned by the rest of the class and the teacher. This procedure will provide an enriched learning experience.

5. Actual classroom tests have demonstrated that this plan of using five to ten copies of this *Alaska* book and one copy of the *Alaska* portfolio, along with traditional textbooks, makes possible a better way to study Alaska and its people.

How to Meet the Learning Needs of Every Child

The editors of this book believe that the secret of successful learning lies in motivating the student to *think*. This fundamental principle has been effectively stated by John Dewey in his book *Democracy and Education:* "The sole path to enduring improvement in the methods of instruction and learning consists in centering upon the conditions which exact, promote, and test thinking. Thinking *is* the method of intelligent learning; of learning that employs and rewards the mind." Our great need is to lead students to think purposefully.

Purpose and Interest

Purpose and interest are the most important elements of thinking. To expect students to read and think about geography without first helping them find a purpose, or an interest, is to invite their failure. The first step in teaching geography should be to create a highly challenging environment that will arouse the natural curiosity of the students. The teacher may create this environment with the help of the proper learning aids. A good filmstrip or large pin-up-board pictures will let all the students of the class see vivid views of life in Alaska. Good geography pictures are a powerful aid for creating interest and developing purpose on the part of the student. The clear, lighted pictures in a good filmstrip that shows vivid, fascinating views of Alaska and its people appeal to every student's natural curiosity. If a filmstrip or a collection of good geography pictures about Alaska is not available, the teacher can group the students in such a way that the entire class may share most effectively all the copies of this textbook that are in the classroom. If the attention of each member of the class is centered on the same picture at the same time, the students as a group can enjoy visual experiences that are almost as satisfactory as those made possible by a filmstrip or bulletin board display.

Successful motivation will bring forth a number of questions to which the class will want to find answers. These questions should be recorded, discussed, and revised by the group. Those that offer a true challenge to the students' efforts open the way for a profitable study of Alaska.

[A portfolio of geography pictures of Alaska size 9-1/4″ x 12-3/16″ has been published for use with this book and other geography textbooks. It may be secured from Informative Classroom Picture Publishers, Grand Rapids 2, Michigan. (*Alaska*—48 plates—$3.95.) Eighteen chapters of loose-leaf text are included for reference use by the students.]

Three Levels of Reading Ability

This book is designed for use on three ability levels, to help the teacher provide for the great differences in reading ability found in the average class. It provides a means for purposeful investigation and purposeful reading by students on each of the following ability levels:

1 — A few of the students will read purposefully only the pictures, some of the maps, and many of the captions.

2 — Most of the students will read the pictures and the captions, the maps, and much of the text.

3 — Some will read with good comprehension all of the text, the pictures and their captions, and the maps.

In each class there will be a few students who will read the book most effectively on the first level only. Each of these students urgently needs a copy of the book for his individual use. The challenging pictures and captions in each chapter make it possible for these students to share many important learning experiences. The teacher will be pleased to observe how much essential information is gained and what thought-provoking experiences are shared by these students, even though they are reading at the first level.

In the average geography class in which Alaska is studied, nearly every student will be able to use this book successfully. Each will read at one or more of these ability levels at various times as the study progresses. All will make the same trip through Alaska, and all students will gain valuable experiences in geography. As a result, all will be able to participate more effectively in group discussion and in group activity, based on an understanding of the important features of the geography of Alaska.

How Many Copies Are Needed?

Each teacher must answer the question: "How many copies of this book are needed for my class?" Each teacher must personally assume responsibility for securing the learning aids that will enable his students to learn successfully. If the class is divided into committees, as described on the preceding page, as few as five books and one portfolio can effectively serve a class of thirty students.

The Editors

CONTENTS

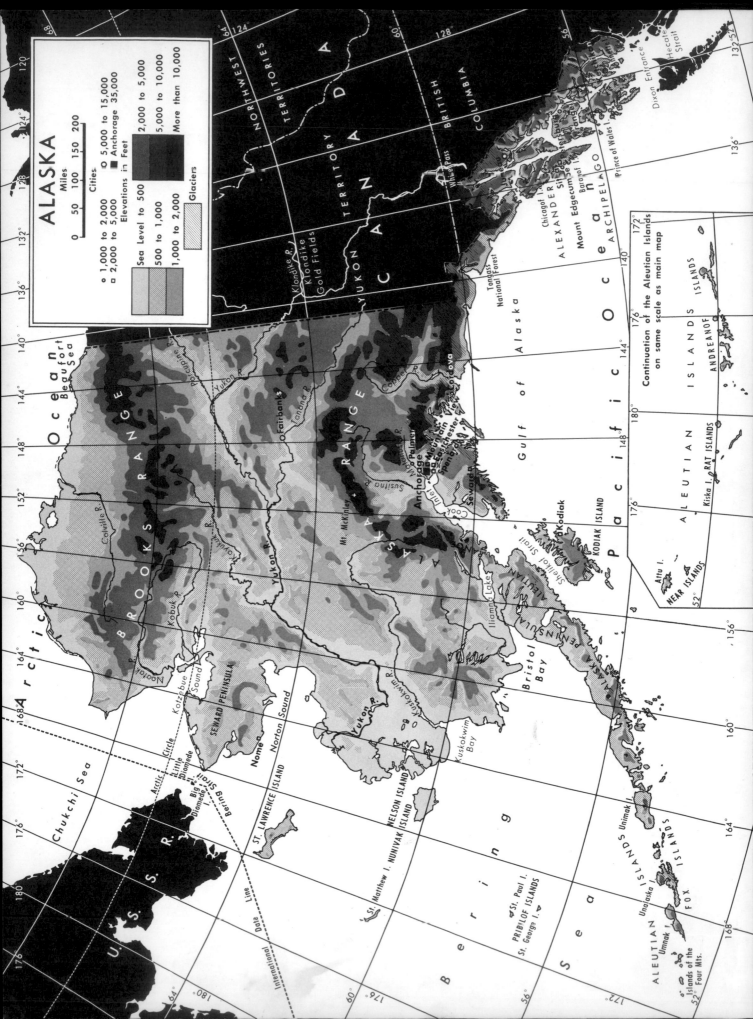

Steamers follow the Inside Passage* in summer from Vancouver,* Canada, to Skagway,* Alaska.

CHAPTER ONE
ALASKA BOUND

Would you like to take a trip to Alaska? We could travel by ship or we could go by automobile over the Alaska Highway. If we wish, we can fly in one of the modern airliners that leave Seattle, Washington, each day. Let's take the most scenic route to Alaska, which is by steamer through the Inside Passage.*

* Please see glossary, page 122.   9

Our ship follows this waterway for hundreds of miles, from Vancouver,* Canada, to Juneau* in Southeastern Alaska. It takes us through the calm, sheltered waters between the mainland and the islands along the coast. In these narrow passages our ship must sometimes reduce its speed. We enter Alaskan waters south of the town of Ketchikan.*

We are now in that part of Alaska called the "Panhandle." It is the long strip of coast that runs south from the main area of Alaska like a handle on a pan. As our ship sails north along this coast, we go in and out between the spruce-covered islands along

Juneau, * like most towns in Southeastern Alaska, is crowded between mountains and the sea.

Many waterfront buildings in Southeastern Alaska are built out over the water on tall piles.

the shore. Sometimes we see a fishing trap, a boat, or a cannery located along a deep inlet. Most of the towns in this section are built on the narrow coast, between the water and the steep mountainsides. Some houses are built on the mountain slopes. Warehouses are built on platforms extending out over the water. These platforms stand on high wooden posts, because the tide here rises and falls as much as twenty feet.

After leaving the steamer at Juneau, we board a plane and fly to Anchorage.* Below us lie the rugged, snow-covered peaks of the mountains along the coast of the South Central Region of Alaska. Many glaciers* move slowly down the mountains and end

11

as walls of ice along the shore. From time to time great masses of ice break off from these glaciers and float away toward the sea. This is an awe-inspiring sight.

At Anchorage we board a train on the government-operated Alaska Railroad and travel north toward Fairbanks.* This is a beautiful trip. We see the fertile valleys of the Susitna* and Matanuska* rivers. We pass through evergreen forests, over mountains, through rocky tunnels, and alongside glaciers. Finally we reach Fairbanks, on the Tanana River.* We are now in the heart of Alaska.

═══════════════════════DO YOU KNOW═══════════════════════

1. Name three ways by which we might travel to Alaska.
2. Describe our trip through the Inside Passage. On the map on page 96, point out the route we followed to Alaska.
3. Locate Alaska's glaciers on the map on page 8.
4. Describe our train trip to Fairbanks.

A glacier.* Many glaciers move slowly down the mountains of Southeastern and South Central Alaska.

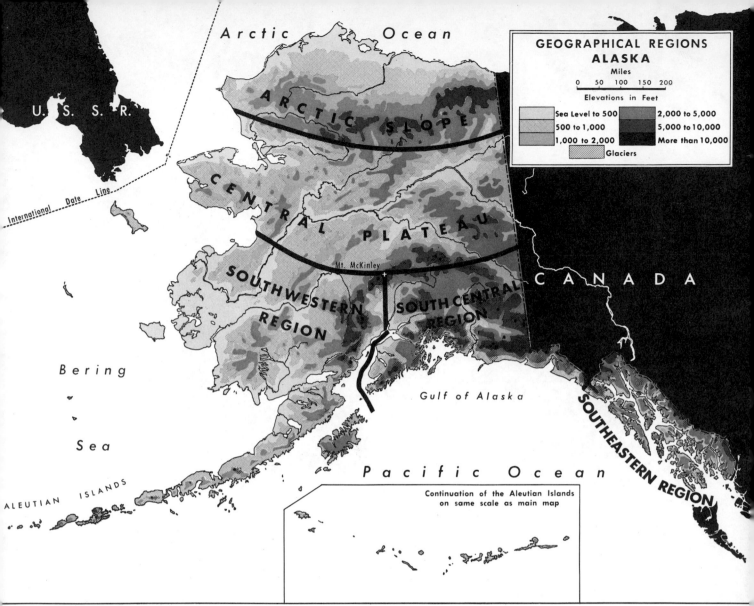

Alaska is the largest state in the Union. It may be divided into five geographical regions.

CHAPTER TWO
THE LAND

Alaska lies in the far northwest corner of North America. It is bordered by Canada on the east, the Pacific Ocean on the south, and the Bering Sea* and Arctic Ocean* on the west and the north. (See map on page 8.) Alaska is by far the largest state in the Union.

* Please see glossary, page 122.   13

Mount McKinley* in the Alaska Range* is the highest peak in North America. It is 20,300 feet high.

Most people who visit Alaska for the first time are amazed to find the summers so warm. The United States Weather Bureau has recorded summer temperatures as high as one hundred degrees in Alaska. The long summer days make it possible in some places to grow wheat, oats, and many kinds of fruit and vegetables. In winter, temperatures in some parts of Alaska fall to seventy degrees below zero.

The Southeastern Region. As we traveled to Alaska by steamer, our ship wound its way through the islands of Southeastern Alaska. This part of Alaska is sometimes called the "Panhandle." It extends about four hundred miles along the coast between Canada and the Pacific Ocean. (See map on page 13.) It is a rugged, mountainous region, with peaks rising from about five to eight thousand feet.

14

The South Central Region. The South Central Region of Alaska borders on the Pacific, and extends about two hundred miles into the interior. (See map on page 13.) This region is sheltered from north winds by the mountains of the Alaska Range.* The warm waters of the Alaska Current* bathe the shores of this region and help to keep winters from being extremely cold. Many kinds of trees, shrubs, and farm crops are grown here. Dairying also is important. Many of Alaska's larger towns are in this region.

The South Central Region. Many kinds of trees, shrubs, and farm crops are grown here.

The mountains of the Aleutian Range* run the length of the Alaska Peninsula like a backbone.

The Southwestern Region. The Southwestern Region borders on the Pacific Ocean and the Bering Sea. (See map on page 13.) In this region you will see few trees, but the ground is covered with grass and patches of small shrubs. The Alaska Peninsula* extends southwest from the mainland of this region. The rugged mountains of the Aleutian Range* run through the length of the peninsula like a backbone. There are more than fifty volcanoes in these mountains, and some are among the largest in the world.

16

The Aleutian Islands* string out eleven hundred miles westward into the Pacific Ocean. (See map on page 8.) These islands are formed by the peaks of an undersea mountain range. These dreary, isolated islands are often shrouded in mist and beaten by storms.

Some of the volcanoes in the Aleutian Range are among the largest in the world.

The Central Plateau. This region is made up of groups of low mountains and the valleys and the flood plains of rivers. (See map on page 13.) One of the rugged peaks of the Alaska Range along the southern border of this region is Mount McKinley.* It is the highest mountain in North America.

In summer, you may see herds of caribou* grazing on the grass and lichens* that cover the high ridges of the Central Plateau. Trees grow in the valleys, and there are some farmlands in the Tanana Valley.* Winters in this region are very cold. Temperatures sometimes fall to seventy degrees below zero!

The Central Plateau is a region of rolling plains, broad river valleys, and groups of low mountains.

Along the coast of the Arctic Ocean* is a bleak, barren lowland region called the Arctic Slope.

The Arctic Slope. In the northern part of Alaska a flat, grass-covered lowland stretches along the Arctic coast. This vast tree-less region is called the Arctic Slope. (See map on page 13.) In winter it is snow-covered and cold. The soil beneath the surface is frozen the year round. In summer, however, much of the ground is covered with grass and wildflowers. These northern plains are sometimes called the "tundras."*

————————————DO YOU KNOW————————————

1. Name and locate the five geographical regions of Alaska on the map on page 13.
2. Using the text and pictures in this chapter, describe the Alaska Peninsula.
3. Describe the Central Plateau region of Alaska. Find Mt. McKinley on the map on page 13.
4. Explain what the tundras are.

Skagway* is built on a long, narrow inlet of the ocean. It is a supply center for miners and trappers.

CHAPTER THREE
SOUTHEASTERN ALASKA

Southeastern Alaska is sometimes called the "Panhandle." This is a narrow region that extends about four hundred miles southeastward from the main part of Alaska. (See map on page 13.) Much rain and snow falls in this region. In the higher mountain valleys are huge fields of ice which have been formed from snow

The Glacier Highway Bridge near Juneau.* This highway is one of the few roads in mountainous Southeastern Alaska.

Modern homes in Juneau, the capital of Alaska. Forests cover much of Southeastern Alaska.

that has collected for many years. These are called glaciers.*
They move slowly down the mountain slopes. (See picture on
page 12.) Some of them reach to the seashore.

A warm current of water, called the Alaska Current,* sweeps
along the coast of Southeastern Alaska. This helps keep harbors
on the coast from freezing during the winter. It also brings this
region a milder climate than many other parts of Alaska. Flowers
and vegetables of many kinds are grown here. Trees grow high up
the mountain slopes.

The towns of Southeastern Alaska lie along the coast. The country behind the towns is wild and mountainous. Roads are difficult

to build in such country. However, the people here have no great need for more than local roads. It is natural that they should travel by sea and air.

Juneau,* the capital of Alaska, is located in Southeastern Alaska. (See map on page 8.) Sitka,* the capital of Alaska until 1906, is also located in this region, on Baranof Island.* This island was named after Alexander Baranov,* a Russian fur trader who was put in charge of Alaska in 1799. The United States bought Alaska from Russia in 1867.

We passed by many of the towns of Southeastern Alaska when our ship traveled north by the Inside Passage.* Let us now visit one of these cities. Ketchikan* is an important Alaskan port city

Ketchikan.* Ports in Southeastern Alaska are kept open all year by the warm Alaska Current.*

of 7,500 people. It is the center of Alaska's salmon-canning industry. Many of the people living in Ketchikan are salmon fishermen. As we wander along the water front, we see nets and fishing tackle on all sides. The harbor is filled with fishing boats. The smell of fish is everywhere. In the summer, hundreds of workers come north from other states in the Union to work in the salmon-canning factories. When the canning season is over in the fall, they return to their homes.

The fishing fleet at Ketchikan. In summer, fishermen catch great numbers of salmon and halibut.*

The wood-pulp mill at Ketchikan. Here giant logs are stripped of bark and crushed into pulp.

The halibut* fleet also puts out to sea from Ketchikan. Sometimes fishing boats sail a thousand miles to the west to find halibut. When the fleet returns to Ketchikan, the catch is packed and shipped to markets in other parts of the United States. Cod* and herring are also found in these waters.

Recently a wood-pulp mill was built near Ketchikan. Wood for the mill is cut in the Tongass National Forest, which stretches four hundred miles along Alaska's southeastern coast. After the

25

logs are brought inside this giant pulp mill, they are cut into twenty-foot lengths. Then they are sprayed with powerful streams of water to remove the bark. Next, a machine called a chipper cuts the logs into small chips. The chips are cooked into pulp. The pulp is pressed into sheets and packed in bales. From the mill at Ketchikan, wood pulp is shipped to cities in many parts of the world to be used in making paper and rayon.

═══DO YOU KNOW═══

1. Find Southeastern Alaska on the map on page 13. What is it sometimes called?
2. Explain why the Alaska Current is important to Southeastern Alaska.
3. With the help of the text and the pictures in this chapter, describe the city of Ketchikan.
4. Tell how wood pulp is made at Ketchikan.

Loading lumber at Juneau. The trees of Southeastern Alaska are made into lumber and wood pulp.

Sitka* Harbor. Hundreds of spruce-covered islands lie along the coast of Southeastern Alaska.

CHAPTER FOUR
THE ISLANDS

There are many islands along the coasts of Alaska. As we traveled through the Inside Passage,* our ship threaded its way past countless islands covered with spruce and hemlock forests. (See map on page 96.) We noticed that many villages were built on these rocky islands.

A village in the Aleutian Islands. * These islands are treeless, wind-blown, and often foggy.

The foggy, wind-blown Aleutian Islands* stretch more than a thousand miles out into the Pacific Ocean. (See map on page 8.) They stand like giant steppingstones connecting America with Asia. These islands are the tops of an underwater mountain range that joins the two continents. There are no trees growing on the Aleutian Islands. However, in places we see stubby shrubs and thick grass. No large animals live here except the livestock kept by the natives. Many of the island people raise sheep.

The native people of the Aleutian Islands are called the Aleuts.*
Their language is similar to the Eskimo language.

It was by way of the Aleutian Islands that the Russian fur
hunters first came to Alaska. From the Aleuts they learned how
to catch the sea otter* and the fur seal. Many of these hunters
were ruthless men who took advantage of the simple natives.
Some, however, settled in the islands and married Aleut women.

Herding sheep. The livestock of the natives are the only large animals on the Aleutian Islands.

Inside a Russian Orthodox church on St. Paul Island.
Russian priests built churches for the
Aleuts of the Pribilof Islands.

Two hundred miles to the north lie the treeless Pribilof Islands.*
(See map on page 8.) In summer they are covered with bright-
green grass and moss. These islands are famous as the summer
home of the fur seals. They are the largest breeding areas for fur
seals in the world. Aleuts live on two of the islands, St. Paul and
St. George.

The two largest islands in the Bering Sea,* St. Lawrence and
Nunivak,* have been set aside as bird and game reserves. Eskimos
live on these islands.

A village in the Pribilof Islands.* The Aleuts* living here kill fur seals for the government.

Farther north, at the point where Asia and America almost meet, there are two rocky islands known as the Diomedes.* (See map on page 8.) Big Diomede belongs to the Soviet Union. Little Diomede, about two miles away, belongs to the United States. Between these islands runs the imaginary International Date Line.* When it is Monday on Little Diomede, it is Tuesday on Big Diomede.

---DO YOU KNOW---

1. Locate the Aleutian Islands, using the map on page 8. Describe these islands.
2. What are Aleuts? In what way are they like the Eskimos?
3. Name two of the Pribilof Islands, and locate them on the map on page 8.
4. Point out the Diomedes on the map on page 8. Who owns these islands?

An Eskimo home on Nunivak Island. * Nunivak is one of the largest islands in the Bering Sea. *

An Indian village. Indians live on many of Alaska's islands and throughout the vast interior.

CHAPTER FIVE
THE INDIANS

Many Indians live on the islands and along the coast of South-eastern Alaska. Let's visit a village of the Tlingit* Indians in this part of Alaska. As we make our way up the village street, we may notice tall, gaily painted poles in front of some of the houses. (See picture on page 34.) These are totem poles, and the Indians regard them with great respect. The totem poles are made from

An Indian boy picking shrimp in a fish house. Today, many Indians work in fish canneries.

the trunks of cedar trees. The Indians carve figures of men, animals, birds, and fish, one above the other into the tree trunks. Each figure tells the story of a past event, or of some hero in an Indian family.

As we look about the village, we see boats, nets, and fishing tackle everywhere. The Tlingit tribe, and other coastal Indians, have always made their living chiefly by fishing. Today, many of these Indians of Southeastern Alaska work on fishing boats or in fish canneries.

35

Totem poles. The figures carved on totem poles
tell stories of past events and
of Indian heroes.

Fish drying on poles near an Indian tent. Indians throughout Alaska catch fish for food.

Many Indians who live in the interior of Alaska are also fishermen. In summer, the salmon swarm up the Yukon River* in great numbers. In places the river becomes so full of fish that the top fins of some stick out of the water. At such places Indian fishermen may set up fish wheels, which are turned by the river current. As one of these wheels turns, its blades scoop the fish out of the water and drop them into a big box. Indian women then clean the fish that are caught in this way and hang them on poles to dry.

The Indians of the interior do not depend entirely on fish for their food. There are usually animals to be hunted. Moose and caribou,* for example, are welcome additions to their diet. The hunters may bring back a large supply of meat from a hunt that will last many weeks. Some of these Indians trap animals and exchange the furs at trading posts for such foods as flour, sugar, coffee, and tea.

In winter, when the rivers are frozen and the land is covered with snow, Indians in the interior usually travel by dog sled. When an Indian has a journey to make, he gives his dogs a good meal. Then he harnesses them to a sled. He cracks his whip, grasps the handle of the sled, and they are off.

─────DO YOU KNOW─────

1. Describe an Indian village in Alaska.
2. Explain how totem poles are made.
3. How do the Tlingit Indians and other coastal Indians earn their living?
4. Using the text and picture on page 36, tell how salmon are caught and dried by the Indians who live in the interior.
5. How do many Indians travel in winter?

An Indian home. Many Indian homes are much like some houses built by white men in Alaska.

In winter, Eskimos fish through holes cut in the ice covering lakes, streams, and the sea.

CHAPTER SIX
THE ESKIMOS

About two thousand years ago, the Eskimos came from Asia to live along the coasts of the Arctic Ocean* and the Bering Sea.* They were short, and brown-skinned. Some people think they were Indians. Unlike Indian tribes, however, all the Eskimos spoke one language, Eskimoan.* These early Eskimos adapted themselves very well to life in the wild, cold country of Alaska.

An Eskimo woman drying fish. In the winter dried fish is one of the main foods of many Eskimos.

They built several kinds of houses. In the summertime all the Eskimos lived in skin tents. However, they all had houses with solid walls for the cold Alaskan winters. Those Eskimos who lived in southern Alaska used logs in building their winter homes, because they could find plenty of driftwood. These houses were built partly underground and were covered with earth. Long tunnels led to their entrances. There was less wood in northern Alaska, and here the earth-covered houses were made partly of stone. The Eskimos sometimes used the curved ribs of whales, or walrus * skulls, to build parts of the walls of these houses.

In an Eskimo winter home. Eskimos in southern Alaska used to build wood houses covered with earth.

Walruses.* The Eskimos killed walruses for food. They also made boats from the walrus hides.

The word Eskimo means "eater of raw flesh." All of the early Eskimos lived almost entirely on meat and fish. They hunted the seal, walrus, white whale,* and other sea animals. For other food, they trapped birds and small animals. Their tools and weapons were very cleverly made by hand. Arrows, spears, and harpoons were made of wood with sharp pieces of bone or stone at the ends of them.

The Eskimos were skillful fishermen and knew where fish could be found. In the winter when lakes, streams, and the Bering Sea were covered with ice, the Eskimos chopped holes in the ice so

41

An Eskimo kayak.* Kayaks are one-man hunting and fishing boats used by many Alaskan Eskimos.

that they could fish. During part of the year they fished from small boats called kayaks.* A kayak was made by stretching walrus hide or sealskin over a wooden frame. In bays or at the mouths of rivers, these Eskimo fishermen caught enough fish to feed their families until the herds of whale or walrus came along in early summer.

For a walrus hunt, Eskimo men had a much larger boat than the kayak. This boat was thirty feet long. It was called an umiak.* The umiak was made of walrus hide stretched over a frame of wood. The hunters carried long harpoons in the umiak, and when a walrus was sighted they started on the chase. If the walrus dove out of sight, the men waited for him to come up, and pursued him again. When close enough, one of the men threw a

An umiak.* Umiaks are large Eskimo boats made of walrus hide stretched over a wooden frame.

The harpoon is attached to the boat by a long rope. Eskimos use harpoons to hunt sea animals.

harpoon. The harpoon had a long rope fastened to it. (See picture above.) After the walrus was struck, the Eskimos killed it. Then the animal was hauled to the boat. If the hunters were near land, they took the walrus ashore and cut it up into pieces. Then the meat was loaded into the umiak, and off they went to find another walrus.

Some walrus hunts went on for days. The Eskimos hunted as long as the weather was good. The walrus herds would not return for many months. The men had to get all the meat they could so that their families would have plenty of food. Only when their

44

boats were loaded did they start for home. When the hunters returned, they were tired and hungry. Everyone was happy, however, for there was enough food for many weeks.

After the men returned from hunting, almost everyone in the village gathered to prepare the meat for drying. When the men killed a whale instead of a walrus, the women cut up the whale meat and boiled the blubber, or fat, into oil. They also cleaned all

After a hunt, the Eskimo villagers gather on the beach to cut up the walrus meat.

Many Eskimos in Alaska still wear warm parkas and waterproof mukluks* in the winter.

the animal skins and made clothing out of them. Little girls in the villages were taught to do this kind of work, too. Eskimo men taught young boys to be good hunters and fishermen.

All the clothing of the early Eskimos was made of the skins of animals and birds. Almost everyone wore fur trousers and a long shirt called a parka. The parka had a hood which could be pulled over the head in cold weather. Eskimo women sewed the clothing with small bone or ivory needles, and thread made from animal

46

sinews.* The Eskimos wore soft, waterproof boots called muk-luks,* which were made of sealskin. Women chewed the leather for these boots with their teeth until it was soft enough to sew.

In the winter, the Eskimos used dog teams to travel over the snow and ice. Their dog sleds, like their boats, were made of animal skins stretched over driftwood frames. Some parts of the sleds, such as harness buckles, were made of beautifully carved pieces of ivory. The Eskimos had a clever way of coating the runners of their sleds with ice to help them glide more easily.

An Eskimo family at play. Today most Eskimos wear some factory-made clothing.

An Eskimo family. Today, many Eskimos live in houses similar to those built by white men.

Eskimo dogs had warm coats of fur and didn't mind sleeping in the snow with no cover. They could run very fast. Some dog teams traveled as much as sixty miles a day.

After the white man came to Alaska, many Eskimos began to copy his way of living. In Alaska today we may see Eskimo villages in which all the houses are constructed of wood. In some of these houses there are shining, modern kitchen stoves that were shipped from factories in other states. Many of the Eskimos wear factory-made suits or dresses under their parkas. In the village of Kotzebue,* Eskimo men use outboard motorboats to hunt white whales. The men in these boats drive the whales into shallow water and kill them with rifles.

The walruses and caribou,* which furnished the Eskimos with food and clothing, have decreased in number. Although the Eskimos still hunt and fish, many of them have found employment in fish canneries and on construction crews. Some of the Eskimos earn their living by selling articles that they carve from pieces of ivory.

Fish drying in the sun. Many Eskimos secure their food by fishing and hunting.

Eskimos carving ivory. Eskimos carve bracelets, necklaces, and other articles from ivory.

When an Eskimo kills a walrus he saves the tusks. Sometimes he finds the ivory tusks of an ancient animal that has been buried in the ground for thousands of years. The Eskimos use great skill in making bracelets, necklaces, and other objects from such pieces of ivory.

───────DO YOU KNOW───────

1. Describe the winter homes built by the Eskimos in Alaska.
2. What foods did most early Eskimos eat?
3. Using the text and the pictures in the chapter, describe the boats and weapons used by the Eskimos on their hunts.
4. Explain how the Eskimos' way of living has changed in recent years.

51

An Eskimo drilling into ivory. The Eskimos once made all their tools and weapons by hand.

Salmon jump a waterfall on their way upstream to spawn* in the waters where they were born.

CHAPTER SEVEN
FISHING

One of the most amazing sights in Alaska is a salmon jumping clear out of the water and up a waterfall. Millions of salmon do this every summer. Sometimes they fall back exhausted on the rocks, but after resting they try again. Most of the fish finally manage to clear the falls. Those that fail die in the attempt.

53

Fishing boats in Ketchikan* Harbor. Many
of the people in Ketchikan are
salmon fishermen.

Why do salmon do this? That mysterious thing we call instinct urges them to return to the same waters in which they began life. Salmon begin their lives as tiny fish swimming about in pools at the headwaters of brooks and rivers. The salmon are constantly looking for food and trying to avoid their enemies. The fish continue to grow in the rivers for one or two years. Then they swim downstream and out to sea, where they remain for the next three or four years. When instinct tells them it is time, the salmon swim back up the rivers. They struggle against the current, fight through rapids, and jump over waterfalls that are in

Setting a fish trap. In winter, a hole is cut in the ice and the trap is lowered into the water.

Emptying a salmon trap. Many salmon are caught in floating traps along the coast.

their way. At last, bruised and battered, they reach the place where they were born. Here the females lay their eggs and the males fertilize them. Then the salmon drift helplessly downstream to die on a sandbar or be eaten by bears lying in wait for them.

The fishing industry is Alaska's greatest source of wealth. More money is made in catching and canning fish than in mining gold or hunting furs. More salmon are caught than any other fish. For many years the salmon fishermen tried to catch as many fish each

A **purse*** **net** is drawn around the fish and pulled together at the bottom to prevent their escape.

year as they could. Most of the salmon were caught in the sea or in the rivers as they were returning to their home streams to lay their eggs. After a while there were not enough young salmon to replace the fish that had been caught. Fish hatcheries* were established to insure a continued supply of fish. Many laws were passed to regulate the time for catching fish, the places where fishing may be done, and the kind of fishing equipment which may be used. Now fewer fish are caught each year, but fishing is still Alaska's greatest industry. In the year 1957, more than 371 million pounds of fish were caught by commercial fishermen. The value of these fish amounted to more than thirty-one million dollars.

Salmon are usually caught with trolling lines or fish nets. Trolling is done in deep water. Long poles stick out on both sides of a trolling boat as it moves through the water. Each pole carries a line and a hook baited with herring. Power scows* come out to the boats at sea and carry their catch back to the canneries.

The nets are carried by small fishing boats that cruise around until they find a large group of fish. This is usually near the mouth of a river when the salmon are returning to lay their eggs. The nets are swept around the group of fish and they are pulled on board.

Salmon caught in a purse net are scooped up in a small net and dumped into the boat.

Fishermen come to the scows to unload their catch of fish and to eat their meals.

Fish traps are also nets, but they are fastened to posts in the water along the shore. The fish swim into these traps, and when once inside they cannot escape. From time to time a scow comes along and collects the fish.

There are five major kinds of Alaska salmon. The big king salmon weigh up to one hundred pounds. Other varieties average about eight pounds, and some kinds weigh as little as five pounds.

Fishermen bring fish to a scow. * Scows carry fish from the small fishing boats to the canneries.

Loading salmon on a truck, which will haul them to a cannery nearby.

Thousands of people are needed to do the work of catching and canning the salmon, halibut,* cod,* herring, and other fish of Alaska. The fishing and canning industries of Alaska employ more than twenty-four thousand people. Many of the fishermen make their homes with their families in the towns and small villages of Alaska. Some workers come from other states in the Union, or elsewhere, just for the fishing and canning season.

─────────────────DO YOU KNOW─────────────────

1. Tell the story of salmon returning to the waters where they were born.
2. What is Alaska's greatest source of wealth? What fish is the most valuable?
3. Using the text and pictures in this chapter, describe two ways of catching salmon.
4. Name some other kinds of fish that are caught and canned in Alaska.

Taking fish from a gill net. The fish are caught when they push their heads into the net.

A **fish cannery** built on wooden piles. Boats unload their fish at the dock alongside the cannery.

CHAPTER EIGHT
THE CANNING INDUSTRY

In Alaska, the canning of fish is done almost entirely by machines. Years ago the fish were cleaned, cut, and pressed into cans by hand. The process today is very different.

When the fish are brought to the cannery, they are unloaded by a machine that carries them, one at a time, along a belt into the main room of the plant. Here they are fed into another machine, called the "iron Chink." It was so named because the first cannery workers were Chinese. This machine cuts off the head, tail, and fins of each fish as it passes, then slits it and cleans it. After this,

The "iron Chink" is a machine that cleans fish after cutting off their heads, tails, and fins.

the fish are given a thorough washing and then inspected by hand. They are now almost ready to be packed into cans. The cans have been shipped from Seattle.

After the fish have been thoroughly cleaned and inspected, they are fed into a cutting machine which divides them into sections. These pieces of fish and the tin cans are then fed into another machine. A metal arm pushes enough fish into each can to fill it.

Canning salmon. Each can is sealed tightly after it has been filled with pieces of fish.

Cooking salmon. The cans filled with salmon are put into a pressure cooker and cooked by steam.

The can then moves farther on and a top is fastened on. The air is pumped out of the can, and the top is sealed tight. The cans are now put in a large pressure cooker, in which the fish are cooked at high temperatures by steam. After nearly two hours, the cans are taken out and allowed to cool.

Most of the canneries are in Southeastern Alaska, South Central Alaska, and along Bristol Bay.* Towns have grown up near many canneries. The people in Ketchikan,* the center of the salmon

65

A floating cannery. Some canneries are built on barges and floated from place to place.

canning industry, boast that their canneries pack more salmon each year than any other place in the world. In addition to its canneries, Ketchikan has cold-storage plants capable of freezing millions of pounds of fish every year for market.

Most of Alaska's canneries are owned by companies or people in other states. One exception is the Annette Island Canning

Company, which is owned by the Indians who live on Annette Island near Ketchikan. Some canneries in Alaska have been built on barges and float from place to place.

Many cannery workers come from outside Alaska at the beginning of the short canning season, and return to their homes when it is over. Some of them, however, live in Alaska all year round.

─────────────── DO YOU KNOW ───────────────

1. Using the text and the pictures in this chapter, describe how fish are canned in an Alaskan fish cannery.
2. Where in Alaska are most of the fish canneries? What city is the center of the salmon-canning industry?
3. Who owns most of Alaska's fish canneries?
4. Where does Alaska get cannery workers?

The cannery on Annette Island is owned by Indians. Alaskans own only a few other canneries.

A farm in the Matanuska Valley. * There are many farms in this valley in South Central Alaska.

CHAPTER NINE
AGRICULTURE

Most of the white men who first went to Alaska were seeking furs and gold. They did not want to be farmers, and few of them tried to grow crops. These white men brought supplies of food with them. When their food supplies were used up, they had to pay high prices for more, which were sent from the United States.

Scientists and agricultural experts knew that good crops could be grown during the short summer season of Alaska. They also believed that if fresh milk and butter were available, the Alaskans would gladly pay well for them.

In 1935 the United States government decided to move some families from worn-out farms in Michigan, Wisconsin, and Minnesota to fertile new land in Alaska. In May of that year, some two hundred families were landed at Anchorage.* They were taken to the wooded Matanuska Valley.* Many of them discovered they did not like being pioneer farmers. They became discouraged and discontented, and returned home. Those who stayed cleared the land as soon as they could, and then they planted their crops.

Cabbages and other vegetables grow very large during the long hours of daylight in Alaska.

During the long summer days, their crops grew rapidly. This new experiment in settlement was a success. Many more families moved from the United States into this valley in Alaska.

Today there are many farms in the Matanuska Valley. Vegetables such as lettuce, cabbage, cauliflower, turnips, carrots, and potatoes grow especially well in this climate. Oats, wheat, and other grains are grown on some farms. There are also many dairy farms, which furnish milk, butter, and other dairy products.

Dairy cows. Dairy farms in the Matanuska Valley supply the people with fresh milk and butter.

Harvesting field peas and oats in Alaska. These crops are often fed to cows in place of hay.

The Matanuska Valley is not the only area in Alaska that is suitable for some types of farming. It is said that the climate of the Tanana Valley,* farther north, is better for tomatoes and safer for wheat.

As the population of Alaska grows, its farming areas will, no doubt, increase. But there are some things which will hinder this growth in agriculture. Farming is expensive in Alaska. In the Matanuska Valley, just clearing the land costs as much as two

71

hundred dollars an acre. New farmers must learn what crops grow best in this climate and how to grow them. An added hardship comes to Alaskan farmers when, during the summer, swarms of mosquitoes and other insects attack them and their cattle. The men protect themselves by covering their hands with gloves and their faces with nets. They drive the insects away from the cattle by building smoky fires in the pastures.

---DO YOU KNOW---
1. How was farming introduced into the Matanuska Valley in Alaska?
2. List some of the vegetables and grains that are grown in the Matanuska Valley.
3. What other region in Alaska has a climate suitable for farming?
4. Explain why farming is difficult and expensive in Alaska.

A truck farm. Many vegetables are raised on truck farms in the Matanuska Valley.

Alaskan caribou.* In summer these animals move to the plains of northern Alaska.

CHAPTER TEN
ALASKAN WILDLIFE

Imagine for a moment that you are sitting quietly on the banks of the Yukon River* in eastern Alaska early on a morning in September. You hear a rustle in the woods, followed by a rattle on the gravel. Soon a big caribou* with spreading antlers steps into view and glances around. With light, springing step he moves to the river, wades in, and the next minute he is swimming away. The rest of the herd follows in line behind him, swimming vigorously in the current. Their antlers are thrown back, and their

Moose live in most parts of Alaska. The bull moose has heavy, flattened antlers.

backbones show along the surface of the water. Their white tails wave like flags. As their feet touch bottom on the other shore, one by one they scramble up the bank and disappear into the forest.

These caribou are on their way south to spend the winter near the Alaska Range.* In the summer they will cross the Yukon River again. This time they will be going north toward the tundras* of northern Alaska. There they will eat reindeer moss* and other plants and grasses which cover the ground at that time of year.

The moose is less beautiful but more lordly than the caribou. His antlers may span five feet from tip to tip. (See picture above.) He keeps to the forest, but toward evening you may see him eating the water plants along some lake shore. At night he may visit

74

a "moose lick,"* where the salty water and mud give him the salt he craves. If surprised, he runs away with giant strides. He swings his legs clumsily from side to side, but he goes very fast.

In the forest and mountain regions of Alaska are several kinds of bears. The black bear loves to visit a garbage pile for a meal. If no one is around, he may make a raid on a kitchen or storehouse. The grizzly bear is much larger and fiercer than the black bear. He keeps to himself. If you are wise you will leave him alone, for he is often dangerous. The Alaskan brown bear is the biggest of all. He is found on Kodiak Island* and on the mainland nearby.

Polar bear cubs. Polar bears that live on ice floes in the Arctic Ocean* sometimes visit Alaska.

The huge, white polar bear lives on the ice floes and in the cold water of the Arctic Ocean.* Sometimes he visits the arctic* shores of Alaska.

The arctic hare, or polar hare as he is sometimes called, is seen everywhere in the northern regions of Alaska. His fur is brown in summer, but in winter it is pure white like the ice and snow. His broad hind feet help him travel over the deepest snowdrifts, into which another animal would sink.

Many kinds of birds fly to Alaska for the summer. In May the wild geese, the cranes, and the ducks flying overhead from the south are a sign of spring. Then come the bluebirds, the robins,

An arctic hare. In winter the arctic hare's fur is white, like the snow. Its summer fur is brown.

and the swallows. In the evening, you may hear the notes of the hermit thrush* in the forest. The white-crowned sparrow sings all night. During the summer in Alaska, you can hear the music of birds at almost any time.

A few of the birds stay in winter. You may see the tiny, red cap of the male redpoll* in the thickets. The hardy ptarmigan* may come down to the valleys to feed on willow buds. He is snow white, and you cannot see him until he flies away. The pine grosbeak,* with his red head and breast, looks like a splash of blood on the snow.

─────DO YOU KNOW─────
1. On the map on page 8, trace the journey of the caribou which is mentioned in this chapter.
2. What kinds of bears live in Alaska?
3. With the help of the picture and the text, describe an arctic hare.
4. List some birds you may see in Alaska during the summer.

Wild ducks on an Alaskan mountain lake. Many kinds of birds fly to Alaska for the summer.

Fur seals in the Pribilof Islands.* Every summer, herds of fur seals swim to these islands.

CHAPTER ELEVEN
SEALING

In 1786, a Russian navigator named Gerasim Pribylov* guided his ship into the foggy Bering Sea.* He came upon a group of rocky islands whose shores were covered with fur seals. These islands were later named the Pribilof Islands,* in honor of their discoverer.

79

A mother seal and her pups. The pups are born a few days after the mothers reach the Pribilofs.

In the spring, herds of fur seals swim to their breeding grounds on the Pribilof Islands. They may travel from as far south as Oregon or California. If they become tired in this long swim, they rest on the surface of the sea, always keeping a sharp lookout for their enemies.

The full-grown males, or bulls, as they are called, arrive on the islands in early May. Each bull selects the place along the shore where his family will live. Later, when the female seals reach the islands, they go to the places the males have selected. Here, during the next few days, their young are born. The bulls remain on shore, jealously guarding their families. They do not leave, even to find food, until August.

The mother seals take care of their young "pups" and find food for them. The pups are given their first swimming lesson when they become strong enough. About the time of the first snowfall, the pups swim away with their mothers to the south.

Ever since the fur seals were first discovered, men have killed them for their valuable fur. After the Pribilof Islands were found to be a breeding grounds for the fur seals, they were killed in such

Drying seal skins. Some Eskimos kill seals and use the skins to make kayaks* and clothing.

large numbers that it seemed the seals would disappear altogether. The female seals were often killed before they could reach land and give birth to their young. Many that were killed at sea sank to the bottom of the ocean and were never recovered. Finally, in 1911, the governments of the United States, Great Britain, Japan, and Russia made an agreement about hunting fur seals. No more seals would be killed at sea, and the United States government would take charge of the rookeries* on the Pribilof Islands.

Scraping seal skins. Only a certain number of young male seals may be killed each year.

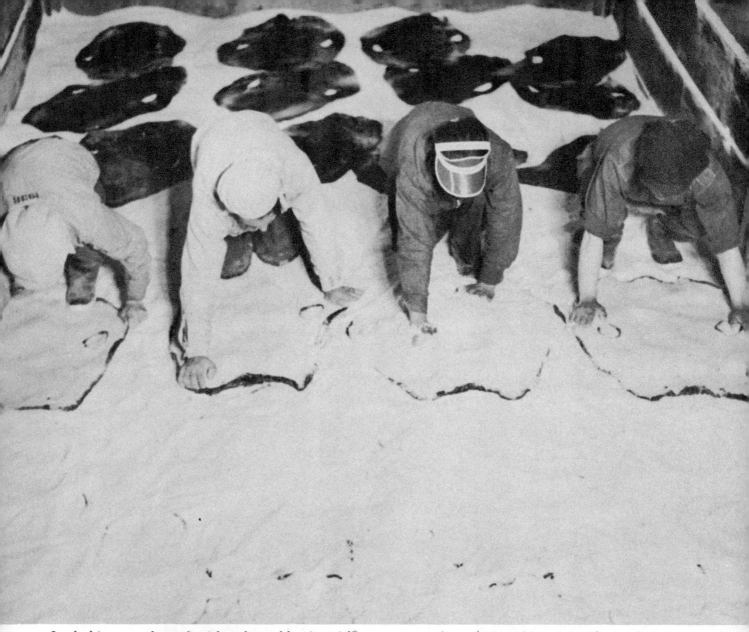

Seal skins are dusted with salt and boric acid* to preserve them during shipment to St. Louis.

United States government agents supervise the killing of the fur seals. Operations usually begin in June or July. Aleuts* who live on the islands of St. Paul and St. George do the slaughtering and skinning. Only a certain number of young male seals are killed. There is always a surplus of young "bachelor" seals, since only the strongest males ever become the head of a herd of female seals. Because of the great care about the number and the kind of seals that are taken, the seal herds have steadily increased in size.

83

After the seal skins are dusted with salt and boric acid,* they are shipped to St. Louis, Missouri. There, they are dressed* and dyed black or brown. Then they are sold to fur dealers at public auctions. This expensive fur is known as Genuine Alaska Seal. It is used in making coats and other fur garments.

─── DO YOU KNOW ───

1. Who discovered the Pribilof Islands? Locate these islands on the map on page 8.
2. Which seals arrive at the islands first? What do they do when they get there?
3. Describe the agreement which four countries made about hunting fur seals.
4. Who supervises the killing of fur seals? What is done to preserve the seal skins?

Packing seal skins for shipment to St. Louis, Missouri, where they will be sold to fur dealers.

A young blue fox. Many of these foxes live in the Aleutian Islands.* Their rare fur is valuable.

CHAPTER TWELVE
FUR FARMING AND TRAPPING

More than two hundred years ago, there were great numbers of sea otters* in the waters around the Aleutian Islands.* These furry, brown animals slept on the surface of the water, and it was very easy for hunters to catch and kill them. Hunters in boats surrounded the sleeping otters and killed them with arrows. They killed so many that there are very few left in Alaska today. Now fur seals furnish most of the pelts* for the Alaskan fur industry.

A fox farm in Southeastern Alaska. Some foxes are raised on farms in Alaska.

Other furs from Alaska come mainly from smaller fur-bearing animals, such as the fox. Red foxes, and a few silver foxes, are trapped on the mainland. Silver foxes are highly prized for their beautiful fur. There are usually many arctic foxes on the Aleutian Islands. They, too, have valuable fur. In the summer these foxes are blue-grey, and they are called blue foxes. In the winter, they turn white and are known as white foxes.

At one time, there were many farms in Alaska where foxes were raised. There are still a few fox farms on some of the Aleutian Islands and on the mainland. Here, the foxes are kept in small pens covered with wire netting, to keep them from escaping. In

An Eskimo trapper. Many Alaskans earn part of their living by trapping fur-bearing animals.

summer the foxes are fed dried salmon. During the winter they are fed any meat that is available.

Many of the Indians and Eskimos in Alaska earn part of their living by trapping fur-bearing animals and selling the skins. They trap foxes, mink, beavers, and many other kinds of fur-bearing animals for their pelts. Beavers make their homes along many of

Removing a fox from a trap. Many animals are trapped in Alaska for their pelts.*

A trapper with two wolf skins. Only the most skillful hunters and trappers can kill a wolf.

Alaska's rivers and small streams. At night one can hear their tails slapping the water when they dive. Muskrats also live near the water.

The big black timber wolves are hard to trap. They follow the caribou* herds so that they may attack and eat any stragglers. When caribou are scarce the wolves may venture close to town in search of food. Something seems to warn the timber wolves of danger, for only a very skillful hunter or trapper can kill them.

DO YOU KNOW

1. How did hunters kill sea otters? What finally happened to these animals?
2. Name the kinds of foxes trapped in Alaska. Where do many arctic foxes live?
3. Use the picture on page 86 to help you describe an Alaskan fox farm.
4. What are some of the other animals hunted and trapped in Alaska?

Panning gold. Early gold seekers washed gravel in pans to separate it from the gold.

CHAPTER THIRTEEN
GOLD MINING

The word "gold" has a magic sound. It was the discovery of yellow nuggets of gold in the gravel along the rivers of Alaska and northwestern Canada that attracted thousands of gold seekers. Most of them came in the hope of getting rich overnight. Others were tired of life in the cities and were in search of adventure, as well as the opportunity to get rich.

The great rush of gold seekers to Alaska began in 1897. People throughout the world heard that large quantities of gold had been discovered along the Klondike River. This is a small stream that flows into the Yukon River* in Canada near the boundary of Alaska. (See map on page 8.) Gold had been found in Alaska in 1850. In the years that followed, other discoveries of gold had been made. But never had gold been found in Alaska in such large quantities as along the Klondike! Many thousands of men came to Alaska on their way to the Klondike gravel beds in Canada, and large amounts of gold were taken from this region. In later years, more gold deposits were discovered in Alaska, and people rushed to these new fields.

One of the early ways to separate gold from the gravel was to wash it in a long wooden trough, called a sluice. A continuous stream of water ran through the sluice while the miners were shoveling the gold and gravel into it. A series of bars called riffles were laid along the bottom of the sluice to catch the gold. The gravel, being lighter than the gold, was washed out at the lower end of the sluice. The gold settled to the bottom. Then the riffles were removed, and the gold was taken out and washed again in a shallow pan. (See picture on page 90.) The miner dipped the pan in water and twisted it from side to side. Any sand and gravel that remained was washed away in the water. Only the shining gold was left.

As gold became harder to find, gravel had to be handled in larger and larger quantities. Today, large dredges are used. A dredge is a barge on which heavy gold-mining equipment is mounted. (See picture on page 92.) Since the dredge must have a pond in which to work, it is usually assembled near a stream. Enough water is let in around the dredge to float it. A network of pipes is driven into the ground ahead of the dredge. Cold water is forced into the ground through these pipes, which have holes along their sides. The water thaws the gravel. Then the dredge scoops up the thawed gravel with a chain of buckets and dumps it into a large drum. The gravel is washed away with water, and the particles of gold are left in the bottom of the drum. As the dredge eats its way forward, it leaves piles of dirt and gravel behind it.

When gold is found in hillsides, the miners cannot use a dredge. Instead, after the ground is thawed, they shoot a powerful stream

A dredge scoops up thawed gravel and washes it in a large drum to find particles of gold.

Water from giant hoses washes gravel into sluices, in which the gold is separated from the gravel.

of water against the hillside. This washes the gravel downhill and into sluices, where the particles of gold are separated from the rocks and dirt.

Although the production of gold has decreased, it is still one of the important industries in Alaska. Millions of dollars' worth of gold are mined each year. Other metal ores are also mined in Alaska. Copper, silver, platinum,* and tin mines produce valuable ores. The tin mines are the only source of tin in North America.

DO YOU KNOW

1. On the map on page 8, locate the region to which the gold seekers rushed in 1897.
2. Describe how early gold seekers mined gold with sluices and pans.
3. Use the picture on page 92 to help you describe how a dredge mines gold.
4. Name four other metal ores that are mined in Alaska.

Anchorage* International Airport. Planes of several airlines fly regularly to and from Alaska.

CHAPTER FOURTEEN
TRANSPORTATION

Alaska's best and most traveled highways are highways of the sky. The vast new State of Alaska stretches over half a million square miles of rugged, largely undeveloped country. Good roads and railroad lines are few, and these cover only a small area. The airplane is the only means of transportation that can serve the entire state. The people of Alaska travel by air more than the people of any other state in the Union.

Alaskans use the airplane as most people in other states use the automobile. Planes carry doctors to their patients, and fly sick or injured people to hospitals. Women fly to cities for shopping or to go to the hairdresser. Sportsmen use planes for hunting or fishing trips, and lawmakers travel by plane to meetings of the legislature.

Along the shore of a lake near Anchorage,* seaplanes line up on the water just as automobiles do in parking lots. These planes are equipped with floats* and can land on lakes and rivers, or on the sea. Many other places in Alaska also provide moorings such as this one for seaplanes. Two airlines in Southeastern Alaska carry on the largest seaplane service in the world. They fly passengers, freight, and mail to and from some of the larger cities.

Planes equipped with floats* land on lakes and rivers throughout Alaska and also upon the sea.

There are hundreds of airports and landing fields throughout Alaska. Planes of many different airlines, both foreign and Alaskan, land at the International Airport in Anchorage * and at other airports. Modern airliners fly regular passenger and freight schedules to and from Alaska. Cargo planes carry bulldozers, mining machinery, and other heavy equipment to places that were impossible to reach before airplanes were used.

Besides the large airline operations, there is a group of brave, dependable men called bush pilots, who operate their own small planes. These men fly to remote parts of Alaska where the larger

Alaska's main transportation routes. Airliners or small planes fly to most parts of Alaska.

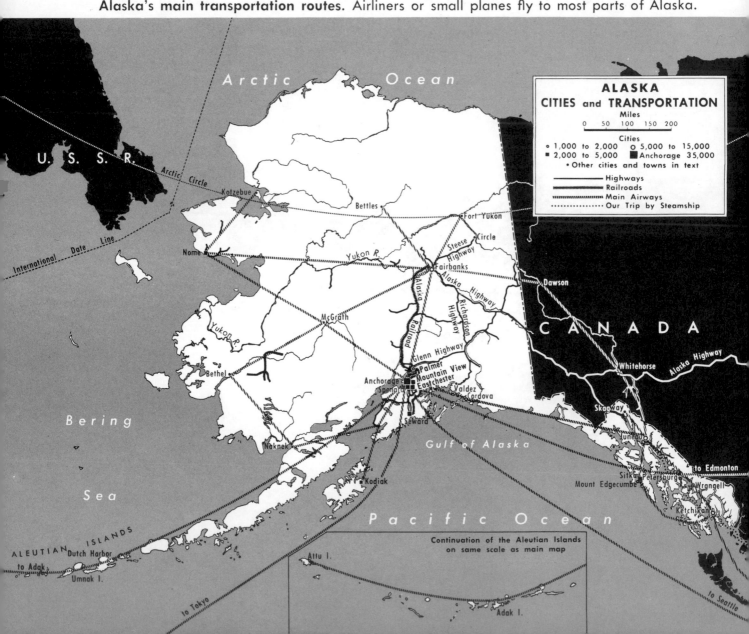

The Alaska Highway. People can travel by automobile to Alaska over this highway.

planes cannot land. Some of them use seaplanes and land on rivers and lakes. Others have land planes that touch down on sand bars, or in tiny clearings. In the winter, the pilots equip their planes with skis so that they can take off and land on snow and ice.

These bush pilots carry freight and also provide a regular mail service to towns and villages that might otherwise be cut off from the rest of the world. Often, they fly through difficult and changeable weather to bring groceries and other supplies to Eskimos and miners. Many of these people might have to move to larger cities if it were not for the services of the bush pilots.

97

Working on the Alaska Highway. This highway was built by the United States Army.

Before the Second World War, Alaska could be reached from the United States only by water or air. Alaskans had little money for road construction, and there were almost no good roads within the country. During the war, however, Alaska became important in the defense of Canada and the United States, and road construction was speeded up. The Alaska Highway was built through the wilderness to link these three countries. New roads were constructed, and old ones within the Territory were improved.

Today, there is a growing network of roads throughout Alaska. Trucks and cars travel northward through Canada over the Alaska Highway to Southeastern, South Central, and Interior Alaska.

At Seattle, Washington, trucks are loaded with supplies for Alaska. These trucks are put on barges and are carried to Valdez,* Seward,* or Anchorage. There they leave the barges and speed their cargos north to Fairbanks,* over the Glenn and Richardson highways. (See map on page 96.) Another Alaskan road, the Steese

Winter on the Alaska Highway. The road is kept open all year round, but travel is best in summer.

Highway, extends from Fairbanks to Circle,* on the Yukon River.* Smaller roads and highways branch out from these main routes.

Railroad lines in Alaska are short, and serve only a small part of the country. The Alaska Railroad was finished in 1923. Its main line carries passengers and freight between the cities of Seward and Fairbanks. A few branch lines were constructed, most of which lead to coal mines. Alaskans are improving their present railroad lines. However, railroads are not an important means of transportation within Alaska as a whole.

A train on the Alaska Railroad carries passengers and supplies between Seward* and Fairbanks.*

Hitching up a dog team. In winter many Alaskans still travel over the snow and ice by dog team.

Ships still travel along Alaska's coasts. Most of these are barges and freighters which carry supplies and equipment to the major ports of Alaska. Although the Alaska Steamship Company has discontinued passenger service, visitors to Alaska may still cruise through the rainy Inside Passage* on ships of other lines.

For many years, winter travel in Alaska was by dog sled. Sled roads and trails led to remote parts of the country, and it was possible to go almost anywhere in Alaska with dogs. Roadhouses along the way provided travelers with food and shelter for the night. Dog teams are still used in some parts of Alaska.

=DO YOU KNOW=

1. Describe two kinds of planes used in Alaska.
2. What highway to Alaska was built by the United States Army?

3. Name the main railroad in Alaska. Locate it on the map on page 96.
4. Use the picture on this page to help you describe a dog team and sled.

A **radio operator** in an Alaskan cannery. Many Alaskans send and receive messages by radio.

CHAPTER FIFTEEN
COMMUNICATION

Today, people who live in or near the larger cities of Alaska may have television sets or telephones in their homes, but radio is the most important means of communication. It brings news, music, and other entertaining programs to people even in remote parts of Alaska. People use radio for long-distance calls. An Alaskan living hundreds of miles from any city can call a doctor over a two-way radio to ask advice about someone who may be ill. He can call for a plane to take a sick or injured person to a hospital. A radio operator in a canning plant in Alaska can call the fishing fleets at sea to find out when they will bring in the catch of fish.

A doctor is called to a lonely cabin by radio. Radio is Alaska's chief means of communication.

Radio became an important means of communication in Alaska after the United States Navy built a number of radio stations there about thirty years ago. These stations were established to serve the Navy, but civilians were also allowed to send messages. In 1934, radio stations were built that were powerful enough to communicate directly with the United States, or with any point in Alaska. These stations are under the supervision of the Alaska Aeronautics and Communications Commission Board. This board also supervises the operation of private radio stations.

This plane was summoned by radio to fly the sick little boy on the sled to a hospital far away.

Delivering mail by motorboat. In summer, boats carry mail on rivers to many parts of Alaska.

The first telegraph lines in Alaska ran between military posts. In 1904, a cable was laid on the ocean floor to make possible direct cable communication with the outside world. Other submarine cables have recently been laid from Alaska to the northwestern Pacific Coast.

Most of the mail reaching Alaska comes from the other states by airplane. Planes also carry most of the mail between cities and villages in Alaska. Until a few years ago, mail to places in the interior of Alaska was carried by dog team in the winter, and in the

105

summer by river boats. Today the service has been greatly speeded up and improved by the airlines and bush pilots who operate their small planes in places where the larger planes cannot land. In larger communities, such as Anchorage* and Juneau,* house-to-house delivery by mail carrier is available. It is more difficult to deliver mail, especially during the winter, to villages in the interior or along the Bering Sea* coast. However, mail service to most of these places is carried on by airplane. Tractors and even dog sleds are sometimes used to carry the mail, but each year more and more of the mail is delivered by airplane.

—DO YOU KNOW—
1. What is the most important means of communication in Alaska?
2. Name some of the ways in which radio is useful to Alaskans.
3. What are the three main types of communication used in the cities of Alaska?
4. Describe how mail is carried in different parts of Alaska.

A plane with skis. Planes carry mail and other cargo to and from many isolated areas in Alaska.

A village school. Many Indian and Eskimo children go to schools built by the American government.

CHAPTER SIXTEEN
EDUCATION

Indian, Eskimo, and Aleut children in more than two hundred native villages throughout Alaska attend village schools. These schools have been built even in the arctic* region of Alaska and on the bleak, wind-blown Aleutian Islands.* More than half of these schools are operated by the state of Alaska. The others are provided by the United States Department of the Interior.

107

An elementary school. Many schools in Alaska are much like those in other parts of our country.

Many of the children who come to these schools have never learned to speak English. In their homes these children have heard their parents and friends speak only their native Indian or Eskimo language. At the village schools they learn to read and speak English for the first time. They learn to write. They study arithmetic and other subjects that children study in our schools. The boys are taught how to make kayaks* and other useful things. They learn to carve ivory. The girls are shown how to tan hides and how to make parkas, mukluks,* and other articles of clothing.

Nourishing meals are served to students at these schools once a day. This food helps to improve the health of the boys and girls by supplementing the native food they eat at home. In this way they can build resistance against tuberculosis* and other diseases from which many Indians and Eskimos suffer.

The teacher is very important to the people of the village. He may serve as the postmaster and the radio-telephone operator. Often, he gives first aid in case someone becomes ill or is injured. Sometimes the teacher even helps the native village storekeeper to keep his records and accounts in order.

The elementary schools and high schools in the larger towns of Alaska are in many ways like our own. These schools are under the supervision of the state government of Alaska. Altogether, there are about fifty of these schools. Eskimo and Indian children who live in these towns attend school along with the white children.

The University of Alaska is located farther north than any other university in the world. It is only a few miles from the city of Fairbanks,* in the heart of Alaska. (See map on page 8.) From the campus, on a clear day, students have a beautiful view of the Alaska Range* in the distance. Students attend classes regularly, even though winter temperatures sometimes fall to sixty degrees below zero.

There are more than seven hundred students enrolled at the University of Alaska. Some of them live in modern dormitories on the campus, and others come by bus from Fairbanks. They study literature, art, music, science, business, education, wildlife management, mining, and agriculture. At experimental farms, students raise different crops to see how well they will grow in Alaska's climate. Some students attend branch colleges of the university in

Anchorage,* Ketchikan,* Palmer,* and Juneau.* The university awards the bachelor's degree to students who successfully complete the regular four-year course. Some departments of the university offer studies leading toward a graduate degree.

---DO YOU KNOW---

1. Where do Indian and Eskimo children go to school? Who provides these schools?
2. List some of the subjects and handicrafts taught in the village school.
3. What are schools like in the larger towns in Alaska? Who supervises them?
4. List subjects that students may study at the University of Alaska.

The University of Alaska near Fairbanks* is the northernmost university in the world.

The governor's mansion in Juneau.* In 1906, Juneau became the capital of Alaska.

CHAPTER SEVENTEEN
HISTORY

The United States bought Alaska from Russia in 1867. This historic and dramatic purchase took place in front of the governor's castle in Sitka,* the capital of Russian Alaska. At first, United States soldiers were stationed in Alaska to keep the Indians under control. In 1877 these soldiers were withdrawn. For a while, the United States government paid little attention to Alaska.

Discoveries of gold attracted many people to Alaska. In 1880, gold was discovered near the present site of Juneau.* By 1884 so many people had come to Alaska that Congress approved a bill

Sitka* was the capital of Russian Alaska and the first capital of Alaska under the United States.

which provided that a governor be appointed for the District of Alaska. The great Klondike* gold fields of Canada were discovered in 1896. Thousands of gold seekers came to Southeastern Alaska on their way to Canada and the Klondike River. Congress then decided that Alaska should have its own laws. One of these laws provided that each town should run its own affairs.

The gold rush brought more people to the city of Juneau than any other city in Alaska. In 1906, Juneau was made the capital of the District of Alaska. In that same year, a representative was sent to the United States Congress.

Alaska became a Territory of the United States in 1912. The people of Alaska had become angry with the United States government over certain coal-mining claims. The Alaskan representative persuaded Congress that the best way to handle the difficulty was to allow the people of Alaska to govern themselves. Congress then created the Territory of Alaska, granting the people the right to govern themselves and tax themselves for the cost of their own government. The first Alaskan legislature was elected and met at Juneau in 1913. However, the new Territory did not rule itself completely. The federal government still controlled the important canning industry and the vast natural resources of Alaska. Also, the governor and the secretary of Alaska were appointed by the president and not elected by the people.

In 1946 the people of Alaska voted to ask Congress for statehood. However, Congress did not pass the bills necessary to make Alaska a state. Ten years later, the people of Alaska prepared a

Juneau is the center of Alaska's government. The legislature meets here to pass laws.

state constitution in the hope that the Territory of Alaska would soon become the State of Alaska. In 1958, Congress granted statehood to Alaska. Now the people of Alaska have all of the rights and privileges that the citizens of the other states enjoy.

—DO YOU KNOW—

1. From what country did the United States buy Alaska? When did this take place?
2. Name the old capital of Russian Alaska. Locate it on the map on page 8.
3. Explain how the people of Alaska gained the right to govern themselves.
4. What city is the present capital of Alaska? Find it on the map on page 8.

Alaskans add a star to our flag. Alaska became our forty-ninth state on January 3, 1959.

Anchorage* is a commercial center in South Central Alaska. It is Alaska's largest city.

CHAPTER EIGHTEEN
THE FUTURE OF ALASKA

During World War II, when Alaska was threatened with invasion, people came to realize that Alaska and its islands were important in the defense of Canada and the United States. Troops

FACTS ABOUT ALASKA								
Capital: JUNEAU						State Flower: BLUE FORGET-ME-NOT		
	Number or Value	Rank		Number or Value	Rank		Number or Value	Rank
Area (square miles)	586,400	1	Population	211,000	50	Date of Admission	January 3, 1959	49
Agriculture*	$3,350,000	50	Manufactures	$40,235,000	50	Minerals	$28,792,000	41
Dairy products	1,604,000	50	Food and kindred products	29,940,000	42	Sand and gravel	8,799,000	24
Potatoes	680,000	35	Lumber and wood products	4,099,000	35	Gold	7,541,000	3
Poultry and eggs	378,000	50	Printing and publishing	2,650,000	40	Coal	7,296,000	15
Forest products	Not available		Fishery products	$ 31,554,000	4	Number of colleges	1	39
*CASH RECEIPTS ●VALUES REFER TO YEARLY PRODUCTION ●ALL FIGURES ARE LATEST AVAILABLE FROM U.S. GOVERNMENT SOURCES								

Fairbanks* is located in the valley of the Tanana River.* It is the largest city in central Alaska.

and supplies were brought to Alaska by sea and over the Alaska Highway. Naval bases were built along the coast. The Army, Navy, and Air Force constructed airfields on the islands and the mainland of Alaska.

Thousands of men in the United States armed forces sailed through the Inside Passage* and across the Gulf of Alaska. American airmen flew over the foggy Aleutian Islands and across

116

lonely stretches of water. American soldiers fought through cold weather, fog, and snow to drive the Japanese troops from the Aleutians. Many soldiers, sailors, and airmen learned to know and to like Alaska. Some of them have returned to this northern land to live.

Alaska's farming, lumbering, and mining industries can provide jobs for more people. More of the coal and metal deposits of Alaska could be mined, with new equipment. The vast forests of

Modern homes in Juneau.* Large towns in Alaska are much like towns elsewhere in the United States.

Forests are one of Alaska's most important resources.

Southeastern and South Central Alaska can provide work for loggers and lumbermen for many years to come. Alaska's swift-flowing rivers are well suited for producing hydroelectric* power. More dams are needed to help provide this electric power for cities and industries. Much of Alaska is still unexplored, and other natural resources may be discovered in the future.

Clearing land. Forests are cleared to provide more farmland in Alaska. This is our last frontier.

Sportsmen come to fish in Alaska's lakes and streams, or to hunt moose, bear, and other big game animals.

Alaska is still a pioneer country that needs vigorous people with strong bodies and determination. Those who love Alaska's land, its variety of wildlife, and its people, will succeed in building a future for themselves. They will find satisfaction in helping to develop this great land. They will help Alaska to become a more prosperous state of the Union.

──DO YOU KNOW──

1. Name Alaska's largest city. Locate it on the map on page 8.
2. How did the United States protect Alaska during World War II?
3. List some of the industries that provide jobs for people in Alaska.
4. What kind of people would make good settlers in Alaska?

A December day in Fairbanks. In midwinter, streetlights are needed during most of the day.

GLOSSARY

Your study of Alaska will be more interesting if you take time to use this glossary.

You should turn to this glossary each time a word that you read in the text is marked with an asterisk (*), unless you clearly understand the word. The letters that appear inside the brackets following each word show you how the word should sound when it is correctly pronounced. The capital letters used in indicating the pronunciation show you which syllable of the word is to receive the chief stress, as: Anchorage *(ANG kuhr ihj)*.

The meaning of each word in the glossary is explained to help you better understand the text and pictures of this book. You will learn much more about Alaska if you will use this glossary.

Alaska Current. A warm ocean current that bathes the coasts of southern Alaska and the Aleutian Islands. It is a branch of the North Pacific Drift, an ocean current that brings warm water from the coast of Japan.

Alaska Peninsula. A narrow arm of land extending about 475 miles southwest from the mainland of Alaska. (See map, page 8.)

Alaska Range. A mountain range in southern Alaska. It extends from the Alaska Peninsula to the Canadian border. Mount McKinley is the highest peak in this range. (See map, page 8.)

Aleut *(AL ee oot).* A member of either of two tribes living on the Aleutian Islands. They speak a language that is related to the Eskimo language.

Aleutian *(uh LOO shuhn)* **Islands.** A chain of mountainous, volcanic islands. They extend about 1,200 miles west of the Alaska Peninsula. (See map, page 8.)

Aleutian Range. A mountain range that extends for about 600 miles along the east coast of the Alaska Peninsula. The mountainous Aleutian Islands are part of this range. (See map, page 8.)

Anchorage *(ANG kuhr ihj).* A seaport city on Cook Inlet in South Central Alaska. It was founded in 1914 as a camp for workers building the Alaska Railroad. Anchorage is now the largest city in Alaska. (See map, page 8.)

arctic *(ARK tik).* Pertaining to the region and ocean north of the Arctic Circle. See **Arctic Circle.**

Arctic *(ARK tik)* **Circle.** An imaginary line around the earth, about 1,600 miles south of the North Pole. (See map, page 8.)

Arctic *(ARK tik)* **Ocean.** The ocean north of the Arctic Circle. See **Arctic Circle.**

Baranov *(bu RA nawf),* **Alexander,** 1746-1819. A Russian fur trader who directed all Russian trade in Alaska from 1799 to 1818. He founded New Archangel, now called Sitka, in 1799-1800. At one time Sitka was the chief commercial center on the Pacific coast of North America. See **Baranof Island.**

Baranof *(BAR uh nawf)* **Island.** An island about 100 miles long in Southeastern Alaska. Sitka is located on its west coast. This island was named after Alexander Baranov. See **Baranov, Alexander.** (See map, page 8.)

Bering *(BEER ihng)* **Sea.** The part of the North Pacific Ocean that lies between Alaska and the Soviet Union. Bering Sea was named after Vitus Bering, a Danish explorer employed by Russia. (See map, page 8.)

boric acid. A mild acid, used as an antiseptic and as a preservative.

Bristol *(BRIHS tuhl)* **Bay.** An arm of the Bering Sea, between the mainland of Alaska and the Alaska Peninsula. It is one of the best salmon-fishing areas in the world. (See map, page 8.)

bush pilots. Pilots who fly small planes to remote places in Alaska. They often land in small clearings, or on sand bars, rivers, or lakes.

caribou *(KARE uh boo).* A kind of reindeer that lives in the wilds of Canada, Alaska, and Greenland. Both male and female have antlers. Their coats are gray or light brown in summer and white in winter. (See picture, page 73.)

Circle. A small village in northeastern Alaska on the Yukon River, about 130 miles northeast of Fairbanks. (See map, page 96.)

cod. One of the most important fish used for food. Much cod is caught off the coasts of Alaska, Norway, Newfoundland, and New England.

Diomedes *(DYE o meeds).* Two islands, located in the middle of Bering Strait, called Big Diomede and Little Diomede. They are about two miles apart. Discovered by Vitus Bering in 1725 and named for Saint Diomede. (See map, page 8.)

dressed. Dressed hides are skins that have been scraped, tanned, and dyed.

Eskimoan *(es kih MOE uhn).* Pertaining to the Eskimos, or to the family of languages spoken by the Eskimos and Aleuts.

Fairbanks. The second largest town in Alaska. It is located in the central part of the state. Fairbanks was founded in 1902 as a result of a gold rush. The Alaska Highway ends here. (See map, page 8.)

fish hatchery (*HACH uhr ih*). A place where fish eggs are kept in jars or tanks until they hatch and the tiny fish come forth from the eggs. Later, when they are large enough, these small fish may be placed in suitable waters, where they continue to grow.

floats. Boatlike frames covered with watertight material. They are attached to an airplane in place of landing wheels, allowing a plane to land on water. (See picture, page 95.)

glacier (*GLAY shuhr*). A great mass of ice that has formed in a region where more snow falls in winter than melts in summer, usually in the mountains. As the mass grows larger it moves down the slopes like a river of ice. If the end of a glacier reaches the sea, it breaks off and floats away as an iceberg. (See picture, page 12.)

halibut (*HAL uh but*). The largest species of flatfish, sometimes weighing several hundred pounds. It is one of the finest food fishes caught in northern seas.

hermit thrush. A songbird of the same family as the robin. It has a brown back and a white breast spotted with brown.

herring (*HEHR ihng*). A valuable food fish of the North Pacific and the North Atlantic. It is eaten fresh, salted, and smoked. In America, young herring are often canned and sold as sardines.

hydroelectric (*HI dro ee LEK trik*) **power.** Electric power produced by the force of rushing water passing through turbines.

Inside Passage. Also called Inland Passage. A waterway of several hundred miles from Puget Sound, Washington, to Skagway, Alaska. This water route follows channels between the mainland and the many islands along the coast.

International Date Line. An imaginary line in the Pacific Ocean, roughly following meridian 180°. It was fixed by international agreement. All over the world, a new day begins at midnight, but each day begins *first* at midnight on this Date Line. The farther west one travels, the later midnight occurs. Therefore, when it is Monday to the west of the Date Line, it is still Sunday to the east. (See map, page 8.)

Juneau (*JOO noe*). The capital city of Alaska. Located in the Southeastern Region. Juneau was founded about 1881. The city has an excellent harbor, ice-free the year round. It has a large salmon-canning industry, and is the trading center of the mining and lumbering region. (See map, page 8.)

kayak (*KY ak*). An Eskimo canoe made of sealskin stretched over a frame of wood or bone. The deck is completely covered except for a circular space in the middle where the paddler sits. The paddler can lace himself in with an apron of skin that keeps out the water. Kayaks are about 16 feet long and 16 inches wide in the middle. Usually they seat only one person. (See picture, page 42.)

Ketchikan (*KECH ih kan*). Seaport town in Southeastern Alaska. A center for fishing, fur farming, and logging. (See map, page 8.)

Klondike gold fields. The gold fields along the Klondike River, a branch of the Yukon. Located in Canada, close to the Alaska border. (See map, page 8.)

Kodiak (*KOE dih ak*) **Island.** An island in the Gulf of Alaska. The first Russian colony in America was established here in 1784. This island is the home of the brown bear, or Kodiak bear. Its most important industry is fishing. (See map, page 8.)

Kotzebue (*KAHT suh byoo*). A village in northwestern Alaska. Located at the tip of a narrow peninsula in Kotzebue Sound. (See map, page 96.)

lichen (*LYE kuhn*). A very small, tough plant that can grow in almost any climate. It looks like moss and is often seen on rocks and old stumps.

Matanuska (*mat uh NOOS kuh*) **River.** A river in southern Alaska, about 75 miles long. It empties into an arm of Cook Inlet. Along its lower course is the fertile Matanuska Valley. (See map, page 8.)

Matanuska (*mat uh NOOS kuh*) **Valley.** The region along the Matanuska River, in southern Alaska. See **Matanuska River.** There are many farms, coal mines, and lumber mills in this valley.

moose lick. A place where salt is found, such as a salt spring. Moose and other wild animals come to such places to lick up the salt.

Mount McKinley. The highest mountain in North America (20,300 feet). Located in South Central Alaska. (See map, page 8.)

mukluks (*MUK luks*). Eskimo boots made of sealskin. (See picture, page 46.)

Nunivak (*NOO nuh vak*) **Island.** The second largest island in the Bering Sea. It is inhabited by primitive Eskimos and used as a game and bird reservation. (See map, page 8.)

Orthodox (*AWR thoe dahks*). Pertaining to the Orthodox Church. This is a branch of the Christian Church to which most Christians of Eastern Europe, Asia, and Egypt belong. It was established in Alaska by Russian missionaries.

Palmer. A village in the Matanuska Valley. See **Matanuska Valley.** (See map, page 96.)

pelt. The skin of an animal, especially a fur-bearing animal.

pine grosbeak. A greenish-yellow bird of the finch family. It lives in the northern pine forests of America and Europe.

platinum. (*PLAT ih num*). A heavy, grayish-white, very valuable metal. It is used in the chemical industry and also in making jewelry.

Pribilof (*PRIHB uh lawf*) **Islands.** A group of four hilly Alaskan islands in the Bering Sea. Often called the Fur Seal Islands, because four fifths of the world's fur seals visit these islands every year. (See map, page 8.)

Pribylov (*PRIHB uh lawf*), **Gerasim.** A Russian sea captain. In 1786, he discovered the islands of St. Paul and St. George, two of the four Pribilof Islands. The Pribilof Islands were named after him. See **Pribilof Islands.**

ptarmigan (*TAHR muh guhn*). A small arctic bird with feathered feet. Its color changes from gray, black, or brown in summer to white in winter.

purse net. A large fishing net, which is set around a school of fish. When the fish are surrounded by the net, the bottom can be closed, much as some purses are closed with a drawstring.

redpoll (*RED pole*). A species of finch living in northern Europe, Asia, and America. The male usually has a red crown and streaked sides.

reindeer moss. A kind of lichen that grows in arctic regions. It is almost the only food of the reindeer in winter. See **lichen.**

rookery. A place where seals come every year to give birth to their young. (See picture, page 80.) Also the name for a breeding place of certain birds.

scow. A large, flat-bottomed boat with broad, square ends. It is used to bring cargo alongside a larger ship, or to take cargo from a ship.

sea otter. A sea animal found off the North Pacific coasts of Alaska. It is about four feet long and has webbed feet. Very few sea otters are left, because too many were killed for their very valuable fur.

Seward (*SYOO uhrd*). A town on the Gulf of Alaska, in South Central Alaska. It is an important ice-free port. (See map, page 96.)

sinew (*SIN yoo*). Also called tendon. A tough cord of white tissue, often connecting a muscle with a bone.

Sitka *(SIHT kuh)*. A town on the west coast of Baranof Island, off the coast of Southeastern Alaska. See **Baranov, Alexander**. (See map, page 8.)

Skagway. A town in the southeastern part of Alaska, about 80 miles north of Juneau. Founded as a result of the Klondike gold rush in 1897-1898. (See map, page 96.)

spawn. The laying of eggs by fish, oysters, and other sea animals. The eggs are also called spawn.

Susitna *(soo SIT nuh)* **River**. A river in South Central Alaska, about 280 miles long. Rises in the Alaska Range and flows into Cook Inlet. (See map, page 8.)

Tanana *(TAN uh naw)* **River**. One of the largest tributaries of the Yukon River. About 475 miles long. The Alaska Highway follows this river for almost its entire course. (See map, page 8.)

Tanana *(TAN uh naw)* **Valley**. The fertile region along the Tanana River. Near Fairbanks several thousand acres of land have been cleared for farming.

Tlingit *(TLIHNG giht)* **Indians**. Also called Tlinkit Indians. Indians belonging to a group of eighteen tribes living in southern Alaska.

tuberculosis *(tyoo buhr kyoo LOE sis)*. A dangerous, contagious disease. It usually affects the lungs.

tundras *(TOON druhs)*. The treeless and often marshy plains of the arctic regions. The ground remains frozen all year, except for the few inches of topsoil which thaw in the summer. Mosses, lichens, and some flowering shrubs grow on the tundras.

umiak *(OO mih ak)*. An open Eskimo boat, made of walrus hide stretched over a wooden frame. It is about thirty feet long and eight feet wide. Often used by women. (See picture, page 43).

Valdez *(val DEEZ)*. A town and port in southern Alaska on Prince William Sound. It is the starting point of the Richardson Highway to Fairbanks. (See map, page 96.)

Vancouver *(van KOO vuhr)*. The third largest city in Canada and chief Canadian seaport on the Pacific. Founded in 1881. Located just north of the border between the United States and Canada.

walrus. A large sea animal that looks somewhat like a seal. Both males and females have tusks. Males often weigh more than two thousand pounds. They are now rare except in the far north.

white whale. Also called "beluga" *(buh LOO guh)*. A small kind of whale, about ten feet long. It is a dark brown-gray when young. Later, it becomes pure white all over. It lives chiefly in northern seas, but is also found in the lower St. Lawrence River.

Yukon *(YOO kahn)* **River**. A river in Alaska and Canada, about 2,000 miles long. It is formed by the Lewes and Pelly rivers in Yukon Territory, Canada. It flows northwest into Alaska, and then southwest across central Alaska into the Bering Sea. It was a major transportation route to the Klondike gold fields. (See map, page 8.)

Index

(Page numbers in this Index that are preceded by "*p.*" refer to pictures.)

ARCTIC OCEAN

Point Barrow

Point Hope

Strait

Diomede Islands

Bering

NOME

St. Lawrence Island

Norton Sound

A L

St. Matthew Island

Nunivak Island

BERING SEA

Kuskokwim Bay

Pribilof Islands

Bristol Bay

Alaska Peninsula

Andreanof Islands

DUTCH HARBOR

Unimak Island

Umnak Island

Unalaska Island

Aleutian Islands